First Pressings

First Pressings

0001

An Annual
Poetry Magazine

ff
faber and faber

First published in 1998
by Faber and Faber Limited
3 Queen Square WC1N 3AU

Photoset by Wilmaset Ltd, Wirral
Printed in England by Clays Ltd, St Ives plc

A CIP record for this publication
is available from the British Library

ISBN 0-571-19517-2

10 9 8 7 6 5 4 3 2 1

The first issue of *First Pressings* is published to coincide with National Poetry Day, an annual celebration that has raised the profile of poetry by a considerable degree. Thanks to this relatively recent institution, for one day of the year at least, poetry is welcomed onto the media gravy train. Bookshops devote space to what is perceived as a difficult and élitist art form; the nation comes together as a school assembly to vote for its favourite poem; poets can again take up their laurel crowns and are re-remembered – after a year in the wilderness – as 'the unacknowledged legislators of mankind'.

But do contemporary poets benefit from the annual festivities? Or are the only beneficiaries, as seems more likely, the publishers, who year after year trundle out the usual suspects for more accolades? The reputations of Kipling, Keats and Shakespeare are confirmed and, hopefully, a new audience is turned on to the charms of the canonical English poets. But what about the poets still to find an audience? It is hoped that, in some small way, this magazine can redress the balance in favour of the poets who miss out on the annual party.

Some of those included in this magazine have already seen their work in print; for others, the title *First Pressings* holds a very literal significance. These twenty-three poets do not represent a common 'school', or 'movement'; they cannot be tagged and filed away under 'n' for narrative or 'd' for demotic; the reader will not find a poetical consensus here or an ordering principle according to which the poems have been arranged. *First Pressings* 0001 is a celebration of the diversity and proliferation of new poetry, a good deal of which, as the biographical notes demonstrate, is being written by a generation of poets who have benefited from the burgeoning resources of creative writing schools throughout the country. The poems that follow are funny, serious, ambitious, compact, sprawling, brazen, delightful and fantastical. They are testimony to the strength and vitality of the imagination. Now that *is* something to celebrate . . .

LEE BRACKSTONE

Contents

Contents

First Pressings

Elizabeth James

Elizabeth James has had poems published in magazines, small-press pamphlets, the anthology *Carmichael's Book* (Morning Star, 1997) and *1:50000 – sixteen short poems* (Vennel Press, 1992). In collaboration with Jane Draycott she has written poetry and sound works for BBC and independent radio broadcasts. She works at the National Art Library, and also writes on art.

The Prince's Mother was an Ogress

My race built to wrestle,
your skull, egg-soft,
slubbered as easily out
as your daddy did when he got you.
Trailing your globby satchel . . .
if you'd been a girl –
but it was first time
lucky, he said, and never came
        near me again.

What are little boys made of?
I remember marzipan
and peaches, the taste
along your neck's furrow, crème
anglaise, and the tip of my pinkie still
dimples pastry after your minute philtrum.
Then anchovy and caviare,
effervescence of pop, and the snip
of elastic in your pants
alive alive-o

*

There's no such thing as an innocent secret –
how did you expect me to take it?

At her improbable loveliness
my lion seat gaped,
those willow loins
your dumpling cherubs
couldn't scrape through –
ladled straight from the stewpot.

If you'd chosen a hearty, horsy gal
with a sense of humour or a mathematical
bent, or if you'd only told me
the tale might have been different.

Too much nothing on an empty stomach
ruins the appetite.
Back in the grip of my maiden habit
I mumble a rote I learned at the clinic,
finger the rosary – how many beans make
saved?
        must have fresh meat

Capricorn

And so I'm left with what I left with, a half-
recognized scent filling the room, a moment
before you might have offered that vivid blossom
drawing us down the midnight path to sit
among the churchyard ghosts like children almost
overtaken first by vague desire

for we were neither children, nor overtaken.
Tethered like constellations to their turn,
the dead to one bruised turf, we shared a breath
of balsam, stayed half-strange, and after dreaming
slept. So the glittering eye of the goat
revolves morosely around its splintered post.

Total Immersion

On the contrary, I'd been around for years.
I was a star, at my zenith, then, in retrospect.
I knew I was good, and believed in the work above all,
but it was beginning to be a strain. Endless
touring was taking its toll. The baptisms drained me.
Police harassed our people, large assemblies were banned.
Self-styled cult-busters came to 'investigate' every week.
Pop journalists mocked the followers as

pathetic nerds who couldn't get on with women.
There were some sad bastards among them, of course,
but I'm not ashamed of that. Compared to someone
we're all sad bastards. At least that sort had no problem
repenting – way over the top, often – but I made them see
it was all to some purpose: they could be forgiven.
What we washed away was their self-disgust.
No, the ones I despised were the upper-class wankers,
along for the ride in their four-wheel-drives,
dipping their toes in the water, looking for legal highs.
I used to christen the rocks in the desert for them:
Freddy! Matilda! the Hon. So-and-So . . .
I had this image: *An axe is laid to the foot of the trees,*
    and each one that fails to bear fruit will be felled and burned.
My work was all about water, but I knew it must
        come to fire at the end.

And then one day he walks out of the crowd.
I'd known him in childhood: our parents were friends, or even
  relations,
and we'd played together from time to time.
The bright boys, they said. Exactly the same age.
But everything I could learn he knew already.
I was impressed, and jealous maybe –
who wants to live in somebody else's shadow?
I never even wondered what he thought of me.
We drifted apart. I began to develop my mission,
he settled down to the family business.
What was he doing, those fifteen, twenty years?
Biding his time, say the wiseacres now,
but suppose he just lost himself there for a while?
Or why would he come to me?

We recognized one another, and were both embarrassed, a
  second.
The next thing for me, it's, like, a thousand volts through my
  body,
my veins are running with scalding oil, I'm weeping holy oil,

ejaculating scalding holy oil.
And I saw him see me know Who he was,
and take it in. And then my profound fatigue,
and determination, and all my secret doubts
were washed away in the greatest single moment of satisfaction
in human history.

He made me go through with it, down in the Jordan,
but what happened then, all the weirdness everyone saw,
was unimportant, even a bit tacky.
It's always that way, the minute you get some recognition
you're tempted to make certain artistic compromises.

I am filled with you
like a little mirror.
In my eye you
are brought to light.

World of Interiors

I live in a New York loft with nineteen windows,
my thirteen-year-old apricot schipperke,
a statue of the Muse of Architecture
looks toward the kitchen island.

I am concerned with the interior as a 'walk-in' still-life.
I was always thought of as the 'artistic child'.
The salon, in beiges, was designed around my own painting,
entitled *Landscape* –

I'm going to make it like a country road
with *trompe-l'oeil* dirt and leaves, my garden and courtyard
being so perfect that they don't seem real.

*

I have no design philosophy. I sleep very simply.
Usually I dream colours, walls, intimacy,

mystery, and other qualities that matter to me
in particular, as a person, and as a Mexican.

The bottom line for everything I do is spiritual.
Life should be more than a series of Styrofoam cups.
I suppose I have always 'seen' light differently.

Next to the fireplace, a seventeenth-century
Zen painting depicts a monkey foolishly
trying to catch the moon's reflection in the water.
What this relates to in Stanley's work is more
the Zen of metaphor.

*

I distribute Cassina, Acerbis, Molteni, Zanotta, Alivar, Arflex, de Padova,
Flos, Artemide and ICF.
I believe that every environment can be improved
and made more beautiful. I like my life.

*

Collecting is not about materialism.
Generally I think that all things have souls.
I may place a Victorian chair next to African drums –
it's the assemblage that still turns me on.

I get rid of possessions almost as quickly as I acquire others.
I am in constant touch with Christie's and Sotheby's.
To the left of the fireplace is a spear
presented to me by a Masai warrior;

a nineteenth-century stone griffin from the Houses of Parliament;
a nineteenth-century Chinese bamboo undergarment
framed in gold leaf.
I think we've done it so it doesn't look like a museum.

*

We do have some things, but they're inside a cabinet
and on the inside of that cabinet it's a tremendous mess.
Outside it's soothing and clear. But when you want
to remember the past, just open up the cabinet, and there it is.

*

Prominent in the hall at Runnymede, my daughter Milica's
Palladian doll's house. I made everything in it myself.
The place was a wreck.
I have located the desk exactly where Colette wrote her novels.

The bed, too, is in the exact position where hers was.
I remember Coco Chanel's flat, and all those books
on their sides, as if they were sleeping.
A real eclecticism cannot be out of a book.

*

Nothing is ever quite good enough.
I realize my quest for visual perfection
makes me demanding of the people I work with.
Of course, I do not believe that all men are equal.

Obviously we never allow ourselves to become bored.
None of us likes isolating people, or people who do.
I suppose one of the reasons I feel like this
is that I live alone.

There is no furniture in the children's rooms.
At the entrance to my office there is a ladder that goes nowhere,
a neutral lobby space –
as does my home, it provides a fine background for anything.

My TV tower is permanently tuned to snow.
In a twenty-foot by thirty-foot room with a fifteen-foot-high
ceiling
I don't want to sleep any more.
At Del Mar I have my collection of model ships.

James Wood

James Wood was born in Scotland and went to Cambridge and Boston University, where he was a scholar working with Derek Walcott and Geoffrey Hill. His work has previously appeared in, among other publications, *Verse, Oxford Poetry, Scratch, Smiths Knoll* (USA) and *The Boston Review* (USA). He lives in London.

The Pool

(for Elizabeth)

It's night. Tearing out of the house,
Leaving your clothes where you leave them,
You race more and more naked to where

The moon floats on its black surface,
A blob of white in a black garden.
With a yell of triumph you feel

The concrete siding and let go,
Sailing through the fall-freezing air
For a few seconds. Hold it there:

You're poised above something
You know nothing about, about
To dip into the unknown –

But you don't care. With another beat
Of the heart it will all be over,
The jig will be up. You splash,

And ripples split the night and all
That's left after a few seconds
Is a slight unsteadiness of moonlight

That bounces off the pool as you stand
Shivering by the back porch,
Laughing nervously, drying your hair.

Alistair McNair

Alistair McNair was born in Glasgow in 1976 and now lives in north Kent. He read English Literature at Exeter University and was head of the Creative Writing Group there. He is hoping to read for an MA in English Literature at Sussex University.

Lake Geneva

Though soon to go, for now, the west
Wind slow to rise, I'll walk to where
The lights are out, to see, at best,
The setting sun pierce night, and stare

Across the beach and harbour point
To where the lanterns start to sway
Upon the pier, as every joint
Warns some expected monster's prey.

Here, I shall see my friends rush out
Before the day, then find with ease
One boat, and call me with a shout

And stop, where one print lies, one track
On which I fell, so deep, the breeze
Has not had time to pile sand back.

The Hare

Funny, how, with fingers almost
Closing our close talk to silent
Touch, we saw, just then, some hare tossed
(As if discarded with intent)

On grass our fingers, minutes past,
Had pulled in ways we'd never known.
Two friends, circled, once encircled
By close talk, now, encircled by

A silent touch they both had said
They'd wanted yet had never known,
Grew far, their eyes searching far past
Each other's eyes, their touch a lie.

Pontius Pilate

They live on the meniscus line,
Pondskaters. They thrive on tension
Between the warm air and the cold.
Now, here I am, where mere mention
Of words would cut skin. I am old.
I spent my morning life, if fine

Weather wished, watching pondskaters,
And grew up with clean hands. Some days,
Yellow dew hung that heavy that
All I held held simply haze.
I would run, sit, perhaps grow fat,
From searching the clear line. Later.

I lie watching hills mirrored in
A lake, and see how much a bulk
Of water can concentrate
On a meniscus line, so thin.
I wash my hands to shake my sulk,
Stretch out, to see my image skate.

Jacob Polley

Jacob Polley was born in 1975 in Carlisle, Cumbria. He's back there now – having nipped about a bit – observing the grazing choreography of local flocks and waiting for his beard to thicken.

The Kingdom of Sediment

I

Rust seemed to bleed downstream
from dumped washing tubs and pram wheels –
the same way we were warned sheep leaked poison
as they lay dead at the source,
polluting the brook's length with corpse,

the taste sharp as broken bottles
if you cupped hands and sipped. Our stream smelled of copper,
the smell that sweats from fistfuls of two-pence pieces,
and bloated to a road's width
when we chased it off cinder tracks

and out from behind houses,
into farmland. There we mud-pied cows –
safe on one side as the herd wobbled, shy,
at the water's edge, half engrossed
in its own image, broken

by lobs that dissolved short.
We saw fences marching through the water
and imagined men wading into the stilled stream
to claim their stretch of its silver,
only to lose it when the current returned and ripped

posts out like teeth. Sometimes we found a door, handles
and all, lying at an angle
suggesting launch had been intended but called off.
We'd shunt it into the stream
and follow it, straining

with sticks to stop its skew sideways
before it wedged between banks. When it stuck
we'd dare each other to step onto the door
and turn the knob, but we were all sure it would swing
open under us – as doors did

when you leant against them, listening in –
and pitch us through to the kingdom
of sediment, where leeches bled your shins
and bicycle-spoke booby traps
ran your feet through like kebabs.

II

To the sewage works at the edge of town
I was led and drowned
while my brother kicked pebbles at a can –
furious when his shots swept wide and swam
under the slurry, stinking up trapped gas
as they were sucked down.

I was drawn by sticklebacks through overflow pipes
into the stream that ran past the works
and picked up the accent of the current
as I babbled down arterial byways:
I found my new tongue
could seep like water around anything.

As the youngest under
I ascended to the throne and was crowned
King of Sediment: I rule suicides
and sea-fishermen who've slipped into fresh water
to escape the persecution of cod
and the gaping spaces of the ocean.

Sometimes I caress familiar ankles –
I have hold of them as the feet paddle –
but my grip slithers
back into the slack when they climb out and shake:
I feel heat running in streams beneath their skin
and long to break the surface.

My sceptre was cast from oxidized flakes of iron –
sifted from the mud-bed – and mercury,
siphoned from the gills of spawning salmon:

the trim around my robes is white-water
and my crown is inlaid with bubbles – caught
while they still held flawless pearls of breath.

The globe I hold is a kingfisher's egg
that rolled into the water as it hatched.
The chick peers from the crack
or lifts half the shell and shows me wings,
sodden at its sides.
It knows no grief, so I tell it stories about above.

Salvage

The shadows in this house are black sails
stuffed with spiders now the wind won't fill them
and they hang from joists of crossed ship's spars
that still hold the curve of a hull
and notches where the ribs of a keel were fixed.

Maybe a mast is among them
but it's pegged to the rest to make the frame
that claimed this house-space from the weather
and no longer lords it over a wet deck,
gulls in the rigging giving voice to its gloats.

Because all wood cut locally has a weak twist
put into it by the corkscrewing storms
that spin off the estuary, men
must have parted the timbers of a beached boat
with the same relish they'd bone a fish:

whoever claimed a wreck would have a house,
built like Adam out of clay and supported
on a skeleton of salted rafters.
The only risk was waking in darkness,
hearing the crooks creak like a ribcage

and becoming convinced a draught was a breath
drawn through the chest of a sailor who'd staggered
this far, flopped onto his stomach
and been hollowed out, his back thatched –
the two slopes of the roof folded over his spine –

his head lopped off and rolled back into the water
and his limbs chopped into the bricks
used to build the walls that gather the garden
to the house, as if to warm it into flower
with its false heart of fire and nests of mice.

Christiane Kupke

Christiane Kupke was born in Germany in 1965. Since 1990 she has lived mainly in Hackney, East London. She is now researching Rudolf Erich Raspe's years at Dolcoath.

Vertigo

Down is an irresistible direction
to fall for. On the edge
of vision, something moves below
the sheer granite. Boulder-weight,
a corner of the eye tips over
legs, pulled by gale-force gravity.

Legs pulled by gale-force gravity,
a corner of the eye tips over
the sheer granite boulder-weight
of vision. Something moves below
to fall, for on the edge,
down is an irresistible direction.

Esther Morgan

Esther Morgan was born in Kidderminster in 1970 and began writing poetry while working as a volunteer at Dove Cottage in Grasmere. She now lives in Norwich, having completed the MA in Creative Writing at the UEA last year. She has just received an Eric Gregory Award from the Society of Authors.

Out of Season

This is all we could afford:
a one-star room
with a dribbling shower,
grey towels,
a thin tablet of soap.

You scrape a chair
across the mock-marble floor.
I hang my flimsy dresses
from thin wire shoulders.
The empty suitcase sags.

At breakfast, we stick to hard facts:
the average rainfall in January,
the local flora and fauna.
The table's littered
with shattered bread rolls.

Outside, the wind piles clouds
like dirty underwear.
We pose alone in front
of scaffolded monuments
for photos we'll never develop.

Days spent in silent museums
learning the island's bloody past.
Bored waiters serve us dinners
of tough, char-grilled steaks.
We leave cold smiles

of fat on our plates.
The night air pimples
my bare arms. Cabs with plastic
dashboard Madonnas
keep bringing us back

to this bed with its hard,
bolster pillow, its sheets
of old paperback yellow,
the crawling caterpillars
of green candlewick.

Lips sealed, we slip
into its tight envelope.
The crab of your hand
inches towards me, shrinking
my nipple to a hard knot.

Sex judders through us
like rubber wiper-blades across dry glass.
We cling to the edges in the dark,
listening to the slow handclap
of a shutter in the wind.

Avocados

I like the way they fit the palm –
their plump Buddha weight,
the sly squeeze for ripeness,
the clean slit of the knife,
the soft suck
as you twist the halves apart,
the thick skin peeling easily.
Naked, they're slippery as soap.

I serve them for myself,
sliced and fanned
on white bone china,
glistening with olive oil,
or I fill the smooth hollow
with sharp vinaigrette,
scooping out
the pale, buttery flesh.

Every diet you've ever read
strictly forbids them.

Neighbours

I request the pleasure of your company.
No need to RSVP,
just kick down the front door,
splinter the safety chain.

Call me by my formal name. *Ms.*
You'll find milk clotting in the fridge.
Apples shrivelling in the bowl.
Help yourselves.

I'm the lady in waiting,
screened behind the shower curtain,
snug as a heart
in a white enamel basin.

I've been listening to you
this past week –
the throb of bass through the floor,
the thump of next door's headboard,

the rasp of awkward keys,
the thwack of a perfect backhand
across a face.
I tell the time in theme tunes.

I'm ready to receive you now,
my hair spread out like weed
in the dark red water.
Be my guests.

Esther Morgan

Love in the Republic

The couples wait their turn,
women twisting rings round
swollen fingers, their throats
hung with silver crosses.
The men's shirts stain between
their shoulder blades. Salt stings
the tips of tongues licking
the seams of thin roll-ups.
Smoke curls from silent lips.

El patrón inspects the line,
palming grimy dollars.
The shack is sun-baked brick.
Inside – a soiled mattress,
naked bulb, frayed wires.
A stifled moan disturbs
the heat. A lizard flickers
from a fading slogan.
The queue shuffles forward.

Andrew Pidoux

Andrew Pidoux was born near High Wycombe in 1974. Last year he completed a degree in Cultural Studies at Norwich School of Art and Design.

The Garden of Good Ideas

Deleuze unwinds his pen across
the page. His deck chair slips.

Guattari laughs and shakes
a flower. It explodes.

They have laced the libraries
of our great houses

with gouged-out tomes
containing brilliant bombs.

Still the looped sky goes
without sound over their heads,

unreadable. Their garden
has gone to seed.

Guattari with a fist of wires
looks up from the cradling dirt.

What happens if I plug
this flower into this flower,

and this other flower
into the proper held space

in the Outside of our garden?
Will it blow me sky high?

Deleuze is dozing. The idea cat
disappears over the wall.

Alison Spritzler-Rose

Alison Spritzler-Rose writes radio drama, fiction, music and poems. She's currently writing a screen-play. She is also the writer of 'La Vie en Rose', a regular column in *The Erotic Review*.

Bukovina

My world is gone: the brothels, rooming houses, the hunt.
I drifted off in a sleeper and the scenery left.
But I remember my dreams. A Jewess who said,
Sir, I know our love is a little thing –
but so are stars, from here.

Bullets too are little things. My limp remembers them.
Our hatreds were holy; we knew why
and whom we fought – the melody and the words.
Now the gentlemen are gone – so too, the wars.

I've been too long in this over-stuffed armchair;
I am moulded to its penitent's horsehair.
My tea has steeped to bitterness

But I see everything, now that the light is as dim
as the moon's reflection in a horse's eye.
I am far-sighted with age.
I see the anger of the oysters
in the pearls on lovely necks. My eyes
water in the cold to make the heavens clearer.

Cows

This Wednesday the cows came home –
a herd the size of England, blanketing
the horizon with misshapen bumps, moving.
They came like exodus on a pit-stop:
some only a few hours old,
still wet on spindly legs,
some still harnessed to ploughs,
old ones with dusty udders
swaying an inch from the ground.
They trampled Bramwell's farm
to a sodden pancake.

I had been dreaming a leopard
but the spots were larger, less close together.
I knew it wasn't a dream
when my nostrils woke to the ammonia sky –
the smelling salts of their administering.
Then the ohm mantra moo,
like a tuning fork – less heard than felt.

By daybreak the media had caught on.
Helicopters circled like angry border collies.
The airlift was a letdown
and the journalists misunderstood.
The SAS gave me tea with whisky.
Have I mentioned the fan mail?
I'm the envy of millions of Indians!

They stayed three days, surrounding my house
and crowding the patches of August shade.
They fertilized and turned my land.
Now I'm growing prize orchids and giant yams.

The Last Place

One step forward, two steps back, trying to establish
what it was, or where it might have been. Because
I know that old wives' tale: *It's always the last place you look*
as if you would continue looking – once you had found it.
As if you would nervily continue to unearth the drawers
of their now useless implements, to braille the dusty shelf-tops,
to flick at the switch (which won't illuminate) to find
yourself tracing your way down the darkened stair
where you will stumble on that final extra invisible step
to lurch headlong into the unending unending
of the last place you look

Alison Spritzler-Rose

Fish People

My father was a fishmonger
My mother was a fishmonger's wife
and I was born with a glistening
of scales down each of my sides.

I used to comb them flat with my sweaty palms.
I used to pretend what it was like to be a rock –
to be able to drown.
I used to lie for hours, just baking in the Sound.

My father worried that the sun
would eventually evaporate the oceans.
He harvested salt
while he calculated each droplet's death.
He mourned each catch.

My mother never fretted
as she chopped off their torpedo heads.
She used to carry sloshing buckets
of the decapitated dead,
humming while she went.
She told fortunes by entrails.
And I used to skim rocks off the pier at sunset.

Each evening the other fishermen
sat drinking beer and shelling prawns while they talked.
And after dark when no one could see
I practised balancing on my fins and learning to walk.

Julian Stannard

Julian Stannard's poems have been published both in Britain and Ireland. He has written a book on Fleur Adcock and is presently the holder of the Crabbe Memorial. Now studying for a PhD at UEA and lecturing at University College Suffolk, he used to teach at the University of Genoa.

Saint Anna's Funicular

When I go down to hell
I will take Saint Anna's funicular.
It will be waiting for me
in the nearly dark of a
velvet-skied Genoese evening.

I will be the only passenger
and the doors will slide shut
with a sublime finality.
It will be an extraordinary occasion,
this journey into eternity.

And in that narrow steep descent
I will be given my last vision
of the city against the sea
and I will pass lighted windows
full of comfort and chandeliers.

Rina's War

Lombardy '43. Fog lingers with fog
and the silent progress of bicycles
has swallowed the wail of sirens.

Rina cannot see the Germans
and the Germans cannot see Rina.
All is lost in the perfection of fog.

Just as the blind can hear the light
Rina cycles off through the rice fields
aware of the butcher, the baker,

the priest, the collaborator, their
silent vehicles swishing past
under the shadow of their breath.

Julian Stannard

At the end of the fog was fog
and a landscape of ghostly bicycles
all ducking and weaving, all hoping.

For nearly two years Rina sliced
through Lombardy with never a collision.
Then suddenly the fog lifted.

David Greenslade

Originally from Wales, David Greenslade studied in Japan before moving to the United States. He now lives and works in Cardiff. He publishes in Welsh and English.

Hi-Fi

When Hugh MacDiarmid died, I was
living in Togoshi Koen. His death
made me think of the poem *Esplumeoir*
so intensely that I went to the
British Council library in Tokyo
and, *like an obstinate jellyfish*, copied
his long obituary from *The Times*.

Later, when I moved to Yamashina –
where I taught English for Berlitz,
until I quit in the middle of a shift –
I hiked, on haiku footsteps,
        persimmon trees in bud,
        cinnamon wafers in the air,
along Testugaku no Michi to
the British Council library at Nishimachi.

It always amazed me how well British Council staff
in Asia resisted going native, since I had
willingly mutated eastward to the uttermost degree.
I knew the library had a record of MacDiarmid reading
and, trying not to bow, I asked to hear it played.

This was Honshu, home of economic miracles,
main island, August 1979, and 'Yes',
there was – available for visitors – beneath
a heap of Greater London *Yellow Pages* – a hi-fi. But,
everyone being British and taken by surprise, no one
let on that the equipment didn't really work.

The record needed a diagnostic wipe;
turntable as choppy as a tar pit;
smoky perspex cover, with a crack in
it as jagged as the north Iwate coastline;
the closet I was led to, a neglected oven
fit only for the crusts of carbon-dated things.

David Greenslade

The librarian rearranged the space as best he could and,
with a look of almost medical concern, left me alone.

Sitting on a swivel chair, with a fractured backrest,
in a windowless storeroom, roasting with dry boxes
brown with sellotape and dull British postage stamps,
I heard MacDiarmid's voice scratched, loudly,
via a clamp of sticky headphones and the tine
of a half-moon volume knob that wouldn't turn.

On this equipment, the year he died,
pang foo, in a suburb in Japan
I listened to C. M. Grieve cry MacDiarmid's *Penny Wheep* –
Wheesht, wheesht ye fule!
    A Welsh ragworm
    dangling a rusty stylus,
    fishing for nibbles
    from the Langholm whale.

Owen Sheers

Owen Sheers was born in Fiji in 1974 and was brought up in London and South Wales. He has recently graduated with an MA in Creative Writing from the University of East Anglia. Selections of his poems have appeared in *Are You Talking to Me?* (Pont Books, 1994) and in the UEA anthology, *Take 20*.

Old Horse, New Tricks

The vet was careful
to place the barrel of his gun
right on the swirl of hair
in the centre of her forehead.

In the silence after the explosion,
she was still for a second,
as if she would stand in death
as she had stood in sleep.

We watched, an audience expecting tricks.
Eventually she obliged,
succumbing to the slow fold of her fall
with a buckling of the crooked back legs

and a comedy sideways lean that went too far.
There was little symmetry in her collapse,
just the natural pattern of pain.
Even her tongue was out of order,

escaping from the side of her jaw,
and dipping to taste the earth below,
like a naughty child, stealing a taste of the cake
before it is served.

Helen Clare

After several years as a science teacher Helen Clare is now taking an MA in Creative Writing at Lancaster University. She performs her poetry throughout the North-West and her work has been published in various magazines.

Biology

Day after day, her heels click on the wooden floor,
the thick cotton of the lab coat rustles
as she reaches for jars behind glass. She knows
them all, the snake skeleton, bleached
slender and white, the rat pinned open like a tent,
the frog displayed and labelled, the skull
with the hole in the forehead, though she jokes
that brains come out best through the nose.

She keeps her scalpel greased and sharp, can slice
clean through the white of an eye of a cow,
pick out the lens with forceps, hold it like a prize
between finger and thumb of her thin rubber glove,
knows the best way to catch worms with soap water
and the best way to kill them, watches them coil,
tight-lipped. In the freezer, there are fish,
the lungs of sheep, the hearts of cows.

Each night she leaves the coat with its nameless smears
on a peg, throws the gloves into a bin.
At home she changes her shoes for boots,
walks the dog, smiles at the way his hind legs tremble,
throws him sticks and stones, feeds him treats
of chocolate and yellow strips, lets him lick her face,
scoops him into her arms, thinking nothing of the mud,
thinking of nothing at all, but his heat, the smell of skin.

16th July 1994 – 'Comet Keeps its Date with Death'*

*Headline from the *Guardian*, Monday, 18 July 1994

I heard the world might end on my wedding day,
began my own countdown
in yards of silk and lace
and champagne roses (seven).

Five hundred billion miles away
a comet fractured into twelve,
spiralled towards a planet
drawn closer – still closer.

Telescopes waited, spacecraft
hung beyond the atmosphere.
I iced a cake, stitched a hem,
slept in curlers.

At three o'clock we met as strangers,
stood separate, side by side, then touched.
The twelve became twenty.
Eighty voices sang 'Jerusalem'.

In the garden I became the hub of the universe;
people circled, brushed against me,
dusted me with kisses, wishes.
I clutched a silver plastic horseshoe.

The sun in its July nearness
shone for me; unblocked by clouds
it stirred the air, warmed my skin,
the pavement. The roses wilted.

Later, taking refuge from the throng,
the stultifying heat of a blinded room,
I sat on a roadside bench, waited
for a fireball on the dark side of Jupiter.

Saw nothing,
took it as auspicious.

The Singing Lesson

My heels dimple the thick polythene sheet,
but leave the Chinese rug beneath untouched.
I tuck my bag neatly beneath the polished table.

She makes me *ning* my scales, feeling the bridge of my nose
for vibrations. When I am more advanced
I will be permitted to *ning-nu*. To do so now
would risk displacing the voice from its seat in the sinus.

She hammers with one sharp-nailed finger.
It is a cheap piano. She does not like my diction,
unstrings the guts from my *g*s. My *ing*s no longer ring.
Later the tape-recorder rattles on mahogany,
My small voice resonates. She is pleased.

She teaches me to breathe, raising the ribs of my back –
a heaving bosom, as she says, would be too disconcerting.
I concentrate, hold my breath, let out a steady stream
that would bend but not snuff a candle flame –
and fart. She is not disconcerted.

I tip into her hand a fistful of silver –
she charges on a sliding scale. In the hall
her stroke-skewed husband gives me sweets,
the old half-sighted dog shuffles his rolling belly into my hands.

She watches me as I descend the terraced garden.
Birds are singing. I hum. I can feel the air in my lungs.
The vibrations in the bridge of my nose.

Sarah Hall

Sarah Hall is a cheeky, fruity little number with a smooth finish, produced in the soggy sheep-shit region of Cumbria, vintage 1974. She started writing aged two in a highly advanced but incomprehensible language, but finally adopted English for tax purposes.

The Tree Stealer

My father's garden fence
had been edging out that way for months,
subtly, a daily inching
of the fence-post trench,
usually a late-evening manoeuvre,
or a crack dawn offensive,
until the unofficial act was complete.

His little kingdom's boundary
stretched around the foreign ash,
older than the other members
in the cultivated plot,
somehow more mysterious and wild,
an ancient still to be standing
long after my father's line is gone from the land.

If I learned tree-language
I could ask how it feels now
to be next to the uniform roses
ideal in their rows,
nearer to the fat hidden worm
in the heart of the apple blossom.

Hello Girl, Hello Boy

We rusted shut in this place,
under the avocado tree, by the new museum.
I pass it daily on the way to my spaceship.

It was fish-trick ridiculous sudden.
Not the slow intestinal trickle of little human cataclysms
or the furious creep of resin
that welds new fingerprints
and sticks hands to the walls like Velcro.

Sarah Hall

It was elastic-snap immediate. We blinked untidily.
The high-vaulted ceilings in our iron lungs
went currant-red and set.
Our eye lenses shuttered once and seized
like the New Metal Age was over.

In the space of two street-seconds
milky galaxies folded and empires fell.
A million woodlice scuttled along the pavement
like escaped wedding rice, avoiding our bare toes.
Our crippled spines sweated ice in sheets.

Even autumn slipped in,
squashed through an invisible trapdoor
and came up into the town fat and purple and quiet.
It installed brilliance in the bark
and risked putting a plaque up for us
that can still be seen on frosty mornings.

Arrangements were made, I recall.
By this time your mother's jam had been removed from my
  cupboard.

A woman got to us with an oil-can
moments before the crowd started handing out rotten tomatoes.

On my arrival home
I peeled back an onion skin
and found you hiding under the first layer.
The position of your limbs
spelled out a word I didn't recognize.

The Amazing Adventures of Carpet Man

I'm belly up usually, four duvets down in the bed, and steering sleep with my knees, like a motorbike to Vegas. Or stirruped, expectant, but with no soft parts exposed. That's when it happens. Nothing manic about the interference, just my brain buzzing like a faulty bulb. It starts with slinky copper singing echoing up the hotel pipes. The floor's been bubbling for weeks. How he comes up is incredible, like being born through a pizza, face first, chest, belly, impacting slowly into the thick air. His hands bring up mozzarella strings and send them pinging from the straw mat. His hands are like black wooden carvings under a church seat. He's looking for the perfect partner to go free-diving through the plush universal carpets of the town. Can he pencil me in? This could be my first or final trip. I never go.

The Swimmers

No synchronized swimming, the new sign insists.
All the city has seen it on screen,
an anti-rust lollipop elbowing down in the sand
as if gravity wouldn't always work.
It says the solo world has won.

The beach is pink and green at this time of year,
warm and corrugated like the roof of a dog's mouth.
There is the residue of light left over from scene one
and a fresco moon flaking all over the shore.
A girl and another are there.
Their boldness is not accidental.
They are perfect on their knees, fizzing like aspirin
after the performance of a lifetime.
It has taken centuries.

In one's belly is a rock, walnut shaped,
humming like a cancer two inches above her liver.
The other isn't strong, she's got tin legs,
but she helps herself to air.
She reaches in, like a brother would, takes the rock,
and skims it hard in the obvious direction,
cracking the letter *y* and the crab-backed religion.

Sarah Hall

Then the two cut a clean autopsy through the shallows,
stride for stride, and diving away from the soil
with stricter technical discipline than a sea-cat,
they vanish into the thin liquid.

Inland, others have suspected their departure,
thinking that they have gone slumming it in an olive grove,
not several strata up in the morning water.
Blood relatives sulk like a group of unlucky oystercatchers.
Not in one irrational, freak-show moment
could they understand the code,
or themselves sneak past the hysterical thought
What if it eats me whole, even my bones?
There are singles-club keepers, alpha-principles,
seafood platters to contend with, they reason.
An absence of damp regret lifts their limbs home.

Amongst the seaweed and subcultures
curling on the ocean floor,
the girl and another are turning prawn circles together,
with tiny vertebrae snapping.
Without even miming the next move
the two simply dissolve
and a fine white powder is left behind by their names.

Matthew Hart

Matthew Hart was born in Manchester in 1974. Co-founder of *ibid*, he graduated from Edinburgh University in 1996, having won the University's Lewis Edwards Memorial Prize for writing in 1994, and is currently a Benjamin Franklin Fellow at the University of Pennsylvania.

In the English Lake District

(against creative writing)

A man has committed a murder
in the English Lake District.
He is strange – says
he's *From Patagonia*,
has thrown his revolver
in the water.

    Describe the lake.
    Do not mention the murder.

Don't look at the wife,
her photographs of picketing;
    the canning factory
    or the knife under the pillow;
the view from the window
of a jumbo jet – Yet

    the lake and the hillside.
    Windsurfers, swans and
    a trout farm your Father –
    once missing – once went,

Say it again:

    Describe a murder.
    Do not mention the lake.

Long after Ovid

May and the soft end of summer,
he sweats in the heat of the greenhouse;

suffering for this seclusion – though
the heat might be good for his skin.

Matthew Hart

There's shade under the tomatoes
– so he shifts there, shiftless,

slowly waiting and falling asleep.
Then Corinna, loveliest of his cousins,

quick through the doorway, dressed
for the weather. All the reverie he needs.

Did she fight for her clothing? Strike
at the mouth so close to her own?

Or lie lightly, slightly drunk and sleepy,
glad for the length of his limbs?

Whatever. – Such questions have a place,
even in the oldest of love poems. And

who'll ask them if not a translator,
translated himself, who's pictured as

an Australasian abroad for the first time,
lost in the woods, stumbling across a greenhouse,

reading glasses dewy with
the closeness of the softer end of summer.

Bicycle

Two-wheelered with my spine striped black
by dirty rainwater, I rode through
Gawsworth – fat sack flapping at my thighs.

Some two years since I'd been here;
and, in the middle distance,
my first school rose then sunk, rose
and sunk with the tightening in my calves.
I have grown since last I came –
my longer limbs, my shorter hair.
My feet are now stable at around size twelve.

I stood on the pedals up Church Lane
and swung left into my still infant street,
swung left again and stopped before
the house that once was mine, the pavement
I'd staked out as sacred ground,
                                        as then
a boy ran in the front door – knees cut,
cane sword shoved skewed in his belt-loop.
His bike lay with its back wheel spinning,
crashed atop a Raleigh. Beaten up.
Drop handlebars and headlamps kissed:
sports frames, touched-up and rusting,
hugged each other – bold before a pedal snared
a spoke and, churning, cast the pair apart.

William Hampton

William Hampton was born in Salford, Lancashire. These days he lives in Colchester where he works for BTCV, a charity-based conservation trust. His poems have appeared in a variety of magazines over the past few years.

Ancient Peoples

The Phoenicians always were my favourites
(one gravitates toward one's opposites).
In this case canny businessmen, well-travelled
proto-capitalists. A self-propelled
quick-minded race forever on the move . . .

ur-poker players who in a perfect groove
just might have sailed around Cape Horn
and made out Table Mountain with the dawn
to sadly say: 'We can't make money here,'
so homewards they'd pragmatically steer.

Betweentimes founding Carthage and Marseilles.
Monopolizing markets north of Biscay –
Cornish tin's a case in point. Oh sharp
mean virtuosi of the Jew's harp!
Polyglots who coined our alphabet
(a *necessary* thing, let's not forget).

Unwarlike. Unlike Babylonia.
Your unimpressed Phoenician shrugs his shoulders:
'That conquest, rape and pillage racket. Man,
it's *nauseous*.' And I, though partisan,
agree – I call myself Phoenician too,
as nationalists go. What type are you?

Letter to My Mother

(after Salvatore Quasimodo)

Mater dulcissima, I was seven years old and your first-born son and
little pony
whose bed you'd make and whose pillow you'd ruff
and scent with eucalyptus plus a sixpence's
silver for a tooth I lost one summer night
flickery with crane flies and important shapes

appearing on the filmscape of a ceiling
of a mid-terrace house that wanted and dreamt
of a telephone and North Sea gas on stream
in the cooker and parades on a coughing TV
of rival birds of paradise. Remember?

I remember you in bed and poleaxed
by depression, weeping and calling for God and Mummy
and kissing my hands with the symptoms of a fever
I carried in my satchel to primary school
where 'An affable boy with a great many friends'
would run to puppy fat in time with a precocious
'understanding of human behaviour
beyond his years', that vanished from his life,
along with the whereabouts of a magical world
where a wardrobe might lead to a winter scene
of mittens and a sleigh across a lake of ice
toward a dam with a chimney stoked by beavers
wearing spectacles who talked and weighed
their every word only in imperial measures.

Mater dulcissima, I wonder what it was
that even then I knew I'd lost, for its absence
haunts me still, as your disappointing son
approaches forty with a liking for ephedrine
and chilly cans of Munich's purest beer
and dissonant music, feeding a computer screen
with words gone lonely walkabout in poems
of Lilliputian consequence I think
as I re-read them, to a soundtrack
of the neighbours' running battles, thriving
through a gossamer wall in a night with a moon
that drips a kicking poison in one, if not both,
of my ears. I've come a short way from your womb

Dulcissima mater, I've sleepwalked a life
for a decade if not more, but don't be anxious,
don't be losing not a minute's sleep,

for worrying about this middling man
will only print a plague spot on the love
of one I know you wanted so and carried
till my birthday after fractious hours of labour
one September when our cries were mingled.

Mater dulcissima, repeat after me
the words last night you told me on the phone –
'*Each day's a joy*', whenever possible.
We'll be compelled to make a parting soon
for good and ill. But let's not think of that,
we've still a thousand reminiscences
to mull over and organize and *understand*
at last. But I'll be seeing you again,
before the millennium; aware my arrival
and my going will be cushioned in your arms.

Richard Skinner

Richard Skinner lives in London. He is a recent graduate of the MA in Creative Writing at UEA. The following texts are from a collection entitled *the light user scheme*, which is dedicated to Pablo's Eye.

the adjuster

As a boy, Pedro had a stutter and loved straight lines.

When he married, he moved to the city for its
railings, striplights, roadsigns, ledges, doorways.

Pedro found he could talk smoothly after his son was born.

When Pablo was a child, he loved his father's singing,
but when it came to shoelaces,
he hid from his father and looked at them, confused.

esther

She woke up and was certain of it, she understood the situation.
She walked all day, distracted. She felt the connection.

She saw the long figure in white. She remembered so she wouldn't forget.

She pictures the shoes of the nurse, the way the mud adheres.
She touched the uniform, dirty and wet.

She began to feel guilty, she felt it was her fault.
The way that lives intersect.

mu

She got up that morning and walked outside.
She went to the square and out of the town, she passed a cyclist who said good morning.

By afternoon, she was under the mountains.
She crossed the bridge with a toothless cat on the wall.
She went into the woods and up to the grave.

She stood for a while, then stepped back and to the left.

Richard Skinner

Lupus Street

The day after she left him, he lay on his bed.
He watched the ceiling and roused himself
only when the sun had set.

Two weeks later, he studied her brush all morning,
pulling out the hairs. Then he washed her sock.

Four months after, he left his room
and smashed every window in the block.

ur-vignette

Her days became unbearably stretched.
Voices were sub-aquatic hums.
Sirens were two-note symphonies.
Breezes were polar storms.

Then, one morning, her skin righted itself.
She knew the gaps in her mind would slacken and fill –
she saw the sun rise, real and full.

post-road downs

She saw the sleek black cars snake along the new motorway
and wondered at the precision of measuring speed.
She saw Orion wink through bits of cloud.

He was late for a meeting at the mortuary. He drove quickly
through the mist and thought about the formation of calendars.
He pictured Ptolemy watching Sirius rise
in the new month of January. Or was it February?

brilliantine

He stopped her in that street and told her
'All this I have seen before'
and asked her to explain it.

She thought about the laws of time,
the day, in the park, when she cried without reason,

the book of inexplicable events he keeps from her,
open and unfairly close to his heart.

tanzania, 1903

That summer, he watches his wife go yellow with jaundice.
He wheels her onto the verandah where, every evening,
she watches the yellowhammers gather in the trees.

One morning, her fever has gone.
He walks outside, not knowing who to thank. He looks around
and sees
fifty-five yellowhammers, dead on the lawn.

Frank Dullaghan

Frank Dullaghan was born in Ireland and has been writing poetry for five years. He has been published widely in magazines including *The Honest Ulsterman, London Magazine, Poetry Wales* and *The Rialto*. He works for an American investment bank and practises martial arts in his spare time.

Crossing

It was some years ago.
The fields had tucked
themselves in for the night
and the sky could hardly
keep its eye open.

There were no markers,
the grey of one holding
spilled into the next.
The high hedges pushed
the road over the hills.

Light cracked a corner.
On the straight
a man waved a lamp, a gun
black in his other hand.
The road stopped

to slow shadows,
balaclavas, eyes,
unblinking muzzles.
At the lowered window
a mouth smoked words,

ordinary words
familiar to an ear
at any border crossing –
'Where are you travelling?'
'Where have you come from?'

But here, out of nowhere;
out of the flat slap
of trees against windscreen;
the settled hum of the mind:
terror.

Not that anything happened –
the licence taken,
noted as British;
my accent – 'Border boy,
home on holidays, are you?'

It was the way the quiet
wrapped about us;
his clean blue eyes;
the slowness of his hand
returning my papers.

Man on the Moon

My father went to the moon
and left me
in our end-of-terrace house
with its chest-high garden grass,
its clothes-line pole that wobbled
and a bedroom full of brothers,

he went to the moon
and I stood in the garden at night,
looked up and wondered
if he was looking down,
if he dreamt of my sisters and mother,
of me and my brothers sleeping
in our large back bedroom,

looked up at the pebble-dashed sky
trying to imagine the face of my father,
a stout man in a spacesuit,
his cardboard suitcase grasped
in his gauntleted hand,
his oxygen strapped to his back,

looked up and blinked the stars from my eyes,
blinked him a message in Morse
that it was time it was over,
that he should put the moon behind him,
shake its dust from his boots
and arrive by rocket, plane or parachute,
stand there beside me
and name me the names of the constellations.

Matthew Welton

Matthew Welton was born in Nottingham in 1969. In 1997 he received an Eric Gregory Award. He currently lives in Manchester where he works in a bookshop.

Parlour Trick

The mirror in the hall reflects the spread
of junk and clutter in the room: the bed
pushed up against the wall, the paper plants,
the drop-leaf table, photos, ornaments.
A square of sunlight lengthens on the floor.

The radio, left on, purrs out some slow
six-eight, the cello with that wheezy low
morendo that's so popular these days.
Roll up the rug, push back the chairs, this place
might make some party: dancing, drinks, the door

open onto the lawn, some darling draped
along the couch, the wall-lights dimmed. Except,
if anybody did come they would find
the pages of the calendar unturned,
the apples clenched-up in the bowl, the bulbs

all blown. The sunshine in the curtain blurs,
the lily water yellows in the vase,
a smell like soil hangs loosely in the air.
The shelves are piled with papers; on the chair,
an uncleared plate, an ashtray filled with stubs.

Wisden

Crossing the rope, eleven on the nail,
the sun harsh, the square as smooth as an egg.
Squinting, his moustache as straight as a bail,
George Summers asking for middle-and-leg.

The sun moving west, the wicket dry, quick.
Picking up odd runs, playing a straight bat.
One ball rising off the seam like a tick.
Struck like a stump, dropping like a spilled catch,

and landing breath-quiet, whites cherry-stained.
The next day, hardly awake, refusing
a doctor, taking the Nottingham train.
Later that season, workmen erecting

a headstone that regrets in inch-high words
The unfortunate incident at Lord's.

Two Hands

Noon
The dizzy girl walked quickly down the beach.

1.05
The roads were slow. The fields were full of fruit.
The smiling boy drove beside the beach.

2.11
The landlord turned the light switch on the wall.
The room was dark, and smelled of winter fruit.
They pulled the shade and watched the empty beach.

3.16
She spoke his name and walked across the room
and did him quickly up against the wall.
They lit cigarettes. They shared a piece of fruit.
He talked. She stared outside, towards the beach.

4.22
The bulky policeman made his usual rounds –
the dairy yard, the parks, the snooker rooms.
He turned and crossed towards the warehouse walls,
the market stands, the yellow fish, the fruit.
He took the quick way back, along the beach.

5.27
He talked about a place they used to know –
his smile got dim, her eyes became less round –
his cousin's house a mile from here, the rooms

he'd decorate each spring, the garden walls,
the ponds with frogs, the yard that stank like fruit,
the fires they'd make with driftwood from the beach.

6.33
She told him as she leaned against the stairs
it's not the only house she's ever known.
She talked about a street where friends came round,
an orchestra, a city where her room
was clean and cheap, with nothing on the walls.
And coming home, her face as bruised as fruit.
And pacing down the beach. The bastard beach.

7.38
For him these furnished evenings never match
that kick, that itch, of shuffling up the stairs
and listening for some voice you think you know,
of knocking once, then twice, then slipping round
the back, of chasing through the basement rooms,
of forcing doors, of slamming into walls,
of striking matches, crouched in crates of fruit,
of watching from the warehouse by the beach.

8.43
The room grew darker. Cars went by outside.
For everything that's wrong, he struck a match:
that ugly mary coming up the stairs,
the radio with songs you think you know,
the tenants' goosy daughters hanging round,
the syrup-marmalade, the breakfast room,
the landlord with a glass against the wall,
the typing-paper bedsheets, polished fruit,
the photographs of donkeys on the beach.

9.49
A panda car drew up across the street.
The bars were full, with people stood outside.
The moon was slim, and dimmer than a match,
and while the smiling boy raced down the stairs

and dogged about as if he didn't know
the road from here, the ambulance pulled round
the front and stopped outside the Chestnut Rooms.
He carried on and waited by the wall
then kicked his way among the rinds of fruit
that washed along the edges of the beach.

10.54
She caught her own reflection in the glass
and stopped a moment, staring at the street.
She sat and smoked. A light came on outside.
She crossed her legs. She lit a kitchen match.
She swore out loud. She shouted down the stairs,
and rattled off about some girl she knew.
She spent a moment sparrowing around
with coins and clothes and cases through the room.
She hung a pocket mirror on the wall
and hacked her hair, and finished up the fruit.
She left, and pounded down the muddy beach.

Midnight
She hurried past the promenade, the pier,
and joined him in the café for a glass
of milk. He took her arm and crossed the street
and put her in a cab. He slipped inside
the boarding house. He tried to get a match
to light. He slumped off down the cellar stairs.

The road was blocked. The driver said he knew
a quicker way and turned the taxi round.

The landlord found the policeman in the room
behind the snooker club. He thumped the wall
until his hands were raw and ripe like fruit.
He took the slow way back, along the beach.

Ruth Smith

Ruth Smith was a schoolteacher until three years ago. Since then she has been writing poetry. She won the London Writer's Prize in 1996.

Tropical Kit

In the end, I gave it away
to a military museum.
It rattled a little in its bag
as I handed it in;
canvas, wood and iron
chafing against each other
while I signed for its discharge.

After the war, we'd requisitioned it;
learnt how to raise
its intractable frame
and link the faded canvas
to its iron couplings.
Then we'd lie on it, rolling
into the dip he'd made

when he lay, parched, on the maidan,
on sweltering nights
that were as hot as days;
or in the cantonment,
vexed with prickly heat;
listening to cacophonous sounds
from the jungle.

From time to time, I finger the gilded
crowns from his epaulettes
or take his service medals
from their slim cardboard box;
but this cumbersome article
took up too much space,
was too much part of his furniture,
and of mine.

Ruth Smith

A Common Predicament

This block's a relic from the old workhouse.
Gaunt behind railings, its windows
stare narrowly from sooty brickwork.

Inside the air's informed with laundry,
polish, disinfectant – and is maintained
at the temperature of bed-warmth.

Each room respires with rhythmic
shudders from machines as I pass
Colposcopy and Breast Imaging

and turn left to see a porter
glissade his trolley down the ramp
that I must stiffly climb to reach today's

assortment of lumbar complaints
and lower limbs. One by one, a woman
in green invites us into her humming room.

'It's been a terrible morning!
Orthopaedics! They're so slow!
Breathe in. Hold it. Now jump down!'

I hand my spinal column to a nurse
and wait, staring at walls, reading
the price list for surgical appliances twice.

'Just as I thought! Thin as worn tyres.
Your back's much older than you are, dear.'
As I leave, I glance at the workhouse chimney.

How tall and straight it's kept,
over the years.

Billy Watt

Billy Watt was born in Greenock and now stays in Livingston. He co-edited the journal *Scotland's Languages*, and his first pamphlet, *Porpoises on the Moray Firth*, was published by Redbeck Press in autumn 1997.

Peninsula of Balance

The swingingness of things, their wheel and spoke
and ebb and flow, I hardly knew back then.
Off school, but with that fading fever when
the world is magnified, blue Woodbine smoke

and Brooke Bond tea (twice stewed) would chase me out
to swing on my grandmother's iron gate.
The rungs chest-high, the stairs precipitate –
I'd spin beyond their cliff-edge, a spent dowt

flicked into quarter-orbit. Then retreat.
A privet hedge, a gatepost and a hinge:
peninsula of balance from which I'd breenge
out at the darkened panes, the empty street.

Beyond the rooftops, herringboned with slate
once strafed by bombers, shipyard gantries pecked
the driven clouds, spun over dry docks specked
with generations: families fixed, in spate . . .

Past three o'clock the town eased into life:
men shrugged home from the bookies and the dole;
bags would be thumbed, feet shuffled back in school;
a factory horn ripped through the sky like a knife

and, listening to the buses shifting gear,
you knew this stolen freedom would be ended
soon – but, launching out again, suspended
in haphazardness, you could just hear

the changingness of things, their tick and tock,
their bump and grind. The world of adulthood
was spinning all around me as I stood
on rungs that were, all, solid as a rock.

Billy Watt

Spillage

Spilling from the floodlit bus
we tramped across the moon-blue ruts,
our Lifeboy caps and belts askew;
I don't remember who it was
– but a clatter, then a gleam
alerted us.

Stashed there by workmen, glinting through
a beaver-dam of planks and branches,
was a screwtop of cheap wine.
I don't remember who dared who
to drink: was it piss or alcohol
or just Irn Bru?

Frankie Coombes was first to test it,
then we all swigged. Electric.
As cold as steel left out all night,
it was fierce and secret, dusted
with an infinite frosted sky –
once only tasted.

The dregs we buried went to waste,
when Frankie put a misjudged pick
through them. We trowelled up the shards,
no longer trading risk for taste;
the distant lights were holes jabbed through
to another place.

Aimée, the Contrary Ceiling-Walker

(In the late nineteenth century she performed by walking backwards
on a polished board, upside down and high above her audience.
Suckers attached to her feet held her up only by atmospheric pressure.)

Impossible funambulist,
I pluck these boards on suckered feet;
beyond my hair's flame audiences
tilt, become a loft of apples.

Women flow from petalled cornets;
men distend like blackened pods.
Only their smoke leaks down this far.
The smallest hover, heaviest.

I balance on infinity.
Above, chairs barnacle a disc
to which all things are magnetized.
A hat, tossed down, parabolizes.

All stairs lead up from where I am.
Bats flutter underfoot; outside
imagined canopies of grass
where horses bloom from spider legs

and spires hang dark like stalactites.
High vaulted bridges scoop out air
where carriages dare gravity
like catapulted coins in shops.

These rubber saucers on my soles
embrace a perfect vacuum;
my faith is in the absolute
pounds of pressure, popped like bladderwrack.

Above, a web to cushion me
from stumbling into gravity –
though falling is an art: the vertebrae
must be arranged just so.

Meanwhile I've cast my net and caught
a world: arms root down to applaud
by fungal growth of timpani . . .
and falling holds no pull for me.

Frieda Hughes

As a painter, Frieda Hughes exhibits both in England and overseas. As a writer, she is the author of children's books and her poetry has been published in *The New Yorker*, *London Magazine* and *The Paris Review* amongst others. Frieda Hughes is married to the painter Laszlo Lukacs and they live between London and Western Australia.

Bird

Flip-top with brain
At the beak back.
Mouth so wide open
Houses would disappear.
Continents cringe, curl their toes
And hang on to their oceans.

Maw with a jaw as wide
As whatever enters. Small mice,
Large cats, or middle-size rats
With twisted whiskers.
Its call hallows the black
That brings silence

And the body bears feathers
In its quiet. Its little soul sleeps,
So small in its twigs.
If it yawns, or belches,
There is a city in there,
With its lights on.

The Favour

The man with the sickle
Is searching for something.
He wades fields of thick gold crop
In house-high boots that do not disturb
A sharp hair of grain,

But the little things
Here him coming.
Rabbits freeze,
Their sad blood is oil
On his metal blade.

Still thirsty
He crossed a continent.
They were crushed in their slums,
In their fallen towers
In their earthquake.

He had to find them fast, find them first;
The old ones fought hardest
They knew him well,
Had seen his face often.
Not one of them wanted him.

Except the suicide in a back room,
Dangling impatiently,
Her shoes off,
The chair fallen.
She was waiting.

It wasn't her time
So he broke the rope,
Gave her soul back,
Forced her to breathe it in
Like smoke.

But she wasn't having it,
She begged to be a sacrifice of no significance
At the end of a twist of hemp.
This time he took the too-soon spirit,
He put her in his pocket for later.

He is so rarely loved
He likes to keep those ones close.

Fire 1

It missed me twice.
The first time at the Candlestick stadium
It caught me in its black rain.
Its sky was sick with trees and gagged
By walls and wooden floors and small dogs,
Swallowed whole.

The second time,
I sat under my tin roof
And heard the ashes rattle in the gutter. Made a wish
with every one, like coins in water.
Its footsteps levelled oat fields and skinned trees,
Quick as locusts, hot as branding irons.

This time it shouted.
And I was out. Furious,
Its voice burst fat beneath tree bark
And the possums froze in their little ash-pose.
Brittle bones pinned black
In their burning hollow.

Still, I didn't hear.
It was louder now. The neighbour's sheep
Were cooked in a field corner, and the chickens blackened
Beyond possessing even a beak or claw to make them birds.
The garage buckled in pain,
Its window dripped from the window frame.

Fire called again.
I was too far away to see
My studio twitch with its disease.
It began with a small red spot that flowered in the floorboards,
Its anemone danced, and the music
Was the crack of wood applauding.

I wasn't in the audience
When fire ate the metal roof like a rice cracker.
Left only crumbs, a dead fridge and bottles
That had mated in their molten passion,
Where once there was the corner of a room
Beneath a sink.

Fire was there when I returned,
Watching from smoke-stumps, and barely satisfied.
In bare, black fields rose twisted squares
That were sheds once. And the studio
Lay perfect on its plot, a fresh-dug grave
Punctured only by its own ribcage.

But the house remained.
All the fire hoses had been and gone
And left it clean. Soot ran right up
To the verandah, where fire had stood calling
And not been heard. Even the water tank
Was fresh.

Fire saw this.
Above the tank grew a vast tree, rotten with life
And crawling things. Fire had hollowed it out.
Still it burned. Fire drew itself together
For a final shout, and the tree exploded,
Left the tank tangled in limbs and emptying its broken cup.

Fire was still laughing
Three days later when, in the dark –
Like musical notes left over from a large opera –
The last flames echoed from their stumps.
Eyes unslept and lips curling,
Still eating.

And now I treat blackened saplings
With water drippers and a plastic tube,
As if the land were some mammoth animal

On life-support for a small cat.
And the last leaves of the tallest trees
Have this new death-voice
As their bloodless shells clatter.

Birds

The poet as a penguin
Sat in his snow-cold, nursing
The egg his wife had left him.

There it was, born of them both,
Like it or not. Rounded in words,
And cracking open its shell for a voice.

In the blizzard,
Beaten up from the arctic flats
Were the audience.

From the glass extensions
Of their eyes, they watched
The skuas rise on the updraught,

Every snap of their beaks
Like the tick of a knitting needle,
Hitching a stitch in the wait

For a rolling head.

Michael Punter

Michael Punter is twenty-eight years old. He has written a number of plays, including *The Wolves* (Faber and Faber). His radio play *Come To Me* was broadcast by the BBC this year. 'Endings' is the first of his poems to be published.

Endings

I

Once I feared the Ice Age. Then
I feared the planet Jupiter. Its
arrangements blocking out sunlight.
Then followed my quite rational
fear of coming drought.

II

So I wrapped myself about with
blankets. Studied hard the mammoth.
I was a nine-year-old survivalist.
But once I'd bound my bone-tent
around, the heat was up.

III

It's in me to dread endings,
I write for a living, after all.
The arctic sheet of my machine
can terrify, burst into flame or
be a door to nothingness.

IV

Four is an unholy figure being
one more than the Trinity. I never
even kiss in groups of four. Once, I
didn't fear the end, but it was dark
in there. I was unborn.

V

It might be time to stop. Take stock
and make provision for the time

I'm without a word to start a line.
But who does that? A longing to go on
is fixed too deep inside the heart.

Neil Addison

Born in 1970. Croupier. Taxi driver. DJ. Prominent member of the Ormskirk intelligentsia. Also owns a novel and other things.

Excerpt from Rimboard

Me dad
cracked up in the army
went to live in the lakes.
Never saw him.
All he left was a manuscript
            on torture techniques
and a translation of the Koran.

I had
the same impetus as all the other tykes
who think they're known by fate:
trawling through the Sunday supplements
and the style magazines
as though they were biblical texts;

devouring *The Face*, *i-D*, even *Harper's & Queen*,
transplanting my untested confidence
into the pictures of a fashion launch
or a movie party, desperate to be seen
by my former friends and to give offence
to my new ones as I snorted up their free lunch.

*

My mother put a contract
on my head while I was under
age. A family one full of aims
            and expenditure.

The kind of one-sided pact
that makes irreparable claims
upon your person, and teaches
you to hate this world with dreams.

For a sworn enemy of tact
a small town comes drenched in vinegar,
its armpits weep with the sweat
of textbook aspirations (the cruellest stigmata
imaginable), and as I've never begged to differ

I went down south –
hitched a lift from a sales rep
who gave me the come-on.
We preened our mutual hunger
without the aid of a map
and drank deeply of our common
tastes, downing each drop.

Afterwards
he offered his analysis –
telling me I wasn't built
to hug the coastline, lost
in a mismatch of beauty.
Not when I had the power
to scandalize London.

Once there
I hired a changing-room in the public bogs,
skinning my anonymity with one fell swoop,
disembowelling the sleeping dogs
who lied to their wives
about their curtailed passion,
calling it 'brewer's droop'
instead of what it truly was.

At first they took me for a pleb
          from the provinces,
but within six weeks my status
had changed to recognition
and I became something of a cause célèbre.

Neil Addison

Those arseholes at the Arts Centre
adored me; I was a handsome little twat.
Just ask Verlane, the poor sucker.
I saw his dick twitch
the first time we met
I knew I had him by the balls.

A fan of notable madness.
A model bohemia in his attic
instead of a train set.
A penchant for set pieces –
opening up another track
in his arm with a cute seriousness
as if it were in lieu of some
satanic debt.

His wife humoured him.
Even her mum and dad
did to a laudable degree.
It was these kid gloves which made
him hate them all. All
he wanted was their protest;
a small buffeting
to make his person feel
cool and slightly holy.

So he came
into my efficient, callous, effortless arms.
Arms which only struck and foraged
without describing tender circles,
or giving alms.

Verlane thought he'd captured
youth when I consented
to his overtures. He thought
I'd consider his heart carefully
instead of picking at it
like a side dish.

I turned on him
the roasted chestnuts
I'd been given for eyes
and as if by magic my whim
became necessity.

He even swore he'd publish
my poems himself if it took his dole
money to do it.

But if Verlane was stupid
his wife was worse.
When he brought me home
and said,
'Before you stands a genius,
he'll be staying in the spare room,'
Matilda held her tongue
like a slice of offered meat
and replied, 'Of course.'

I dragged him round clubland
every night for weeks
until Friday and Saturday
were no longer the weekend,
just a pair of liars. And with such
a catch on his arm he was rightly pleased.
I lured him out of himself
and turned him on to Es
while love gave him clearance
to joyously offend.

Matilda realized
that things were completely fucked up.
She went to stay with her parents.

Life had never adhered to her plan:

when she got pregnant she had hoped
the baby would prove her personal messiah.
She lay there for nine months
trussed up in their boudoir,
her belly miserable, a sparkle in her eyes.

It was only two weeks
since she'd given him 'One Last Chance'
            again
after the last time
when he'd thrown their sprog against
the bedroom wall as if
            it were a blunt dart,
screaming and flightless.

The main difference between me and Verlane
was that he believed it was possible
            to go too far
to give up too much:
it wasn't long before
he started pining for the rancid teat
of his wife again, although it was out of date
and yielded nothing but soapy water.

Verlane's desire for freedom
was more of an itch,
and his soul at heart was bourgeois;

even though Matilda's body
was an allotment for bruises
he didn't have the heart
            to call it a day.

He sent her a stream of excuses
and phone calls skilfully
punctuated with that lifeless remark:
'Look Matilda, what do you want me to say?'

'I want you to stop that scally
using our home as a playground.
I want you to ring the social services
and get him sent back where
he came from.'

But she still didn't know
I was a pain in his arse.
She knew nothing of the vices
we'd achieved nor had she found
the lengths of dried-out come
which we'd grafted onto the sofa.
Thankfully the case remained closed
and the curdled tally of our farce
stayed mum.

Nonetheless I went back up north
for a while. Verlane got one of those
jobs for idiots, commission only.
After his one-day seminar –
anticipating a grand a week –
he hit the road.

He didn't get very far
with his cold calling.
In fact it took him
a month to make a pony,
and that was money owed
to McManus and the Greek.

I couldn't think to write.
Even the giro forms confounded me.
If you swallow heaven each night
what on earth is left?

'God's gone so get this down you.'
She gestured to a tablet, a yellow
contract, resting quietly in her palm.

Neil Addison

'Do it and don't look back.'

i did and in ecstasy was wrapt,
flapping like a pierced cockerel.
The seed burst in my fallow
mind, and it blazed with lobes
of fruit, ropes of tobacco,
shards of clementine.
120 beats were tailored into a minute
and the dancefloor was joined in spasmodic communion.

i saw pleasures unexisting